Phonic **Reading Prog**

A Treat for Emily Elizabeth

by Janelle Cherrington
Illustrated by Mark Marderosian

Based on the books by Norman Bridwell

SCHOLASTIC INC.
New York Toronto London Auckland Sydney
Mexico City New Delhi Hong Kong Buenos Aires

Clifford, Cleo, and
T-Bone run to the beach.

They are there to work.

Clifford wants to get
Emily Elizabeth a treat.

He wants to get her
a seashell.

The dogs look all over.

They work as a team.

"Look at this shell, Clifford!" says T-Bone. "It is neat."

Clifford looks.

The shell is big—and very clean.

"Thank you, T-Bone. Nice work!" Clifford says.

Cleo looks.

She sets her ear on the shell so she can hear the sea.

Then Cleo squeals!

"Ouch! That is mean," she says.

"This shell is my only home," says a crab. "Please leave it alone."

Clifford is sad.

Can he still give
Emily Elizabeth a treat?

Yes!
Clifford can!